WISE Activity Spaces

Inspiration & Information for the Do-It-Yourselfer

Laura F. Gross

CREATIVE
PUBLISHING
international

CHANHASSEN, MINNESOTA

www.creativepub.com

Copyright © 2004
Creative Publishing international, Inc.
18705 Lake Drive East
Chanhassen, Minnesota 55317
1-800-328-3895
www.creativepub.com
All rights reserved

Printed on American Paper by: Quebecor World

10 9 8 7 6 5 4 3 2 1

President/CEO: Ken Fund
Vice President/Publisher: Linda Ball
Vice President/Retail Sales & Marketing: Kevin Haas

Executive Editor: Bryan Trandem
Creative Director: Tim Himsel
Managing Editor: Michelle Skudlarek
Editorial Director: Jerri Farris

Author: Laura F. Gross
Copy Editor: Linnéa Christensen
Art Director: Kari Johnston
Mac Designer: Jon Simpson
Technical Illustrator: Earl Slack
Project Managers: Julie Caruso, Tracy Stanley
Photo Researcher: Julie Caruso
Production Manager: Helga Thelen

IdeaWise: Activity Spaces

Library of Congress
Cataloging-in-Publication Data

ISBN 1-58923-157-0

Table of Contents

Introduction

We begin with the premise that any activity we do in the home should have a designated space in which to do it: Sleep happens in bedrooms; kitchens are for cooking; baths take place in bathrooms. Those are the basics, and most of us have them covered.

This book is about carving out physical space for all the other activities we yearn to indulge. We want to quilt, weld, saw, tinker, read, relax, sweat, chill out, surf the Internet, repot the dahlias, compose, compute, compare, catch last season's reality TV hit on DVD, and play with Junior's train set. We want to do so in rapid succession, and within the safety and comfort of our own homes. That's really not asking so much. So why can't most of us swing it?

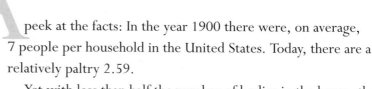

A peek at the facts: In the year 1900 there were, on average, 7 people per household in the United States. Today, there are a relatively paltry 2.59.

Yet with less than half the number of bodies in the home, the physical size of single-family houses in our country has more than doubled in the last 50 years. The average new home built today has slightly over 2,200 finished square feet.

Fewer people, more space. Those are the facts. Why, then, the space issues?

There are a couple factors to consider: First, while the rooms on new houses tend to be bigger, the basic blueprint hasn't evolved with our lifestyles. We have formal dining rooms but usually eat in the kitchen; living rooms sit empty while everyone crams into the family room; the guest bedroom (not unlike the guest towel) goes unused 98 percent of the time.

Just as there are rooms that don't fit our lifestyles, our lifestyles don't fit our rooms. Think about this: Although close to 60 percent of U.S. households have a home computer, almost none of our homes were designed with a functional, efficient space in which to use one.

Well over one-third of us have a dog, but where's Poochie when we're away for a few hours? Usually baby-gated into the kitchen or hogging valuable floor space in a portable wire cage. As common as pets are, most of us have no designated spot for feeding, grooming, and housing them.

One last thing: Where are your books? Your videos and DVDs? Your CDs? Where do you set down the mail when you come home in the evening? Where do you sort out the junk mail? If your house is like most, loose items end up scattered, piled, and toppling due to lack of designated, organized space. We need to think about the odds and ends in much the same way collectors view their collections: If it's important enough to keep, it deserves designated space.

The Money vs. Creativity tradeoff:

For our readers with unlimited budgets, finding space for every activity is as simple as adding on (and on, and on...). If you find yourself in this category, you probably don't need this book (but we urge you to buy a copy for a less fortunate friend).

For the rest of us, this book is proof of the inverse relationship between creativity and budget vis-à-vis activity spaces. The greater the creativity, the smaller the budget necessary to find the space for every little thing you want—and, darn it, deserve—to do in your own home.

We'll show you how to make use of nooks, alcoves, corners, hallways, stairways, lofts, niches, and every other non-room in the house. We'll explore converting dark basements, dusty attics, and garages into functional space.

This book will inspire your inner interior designer while feeding the left side of your brain the hard, cold information it craves (costs, codes, etc.).

Most importantly, you'll arrive at this enlightened state of mind without necessarily enlarging the existing footprint of your house!

The cost of adding space—as opposed to converting space—can be prohibitive. Figure the expense of excavating land, pouring foundation, framing, wiring, insulating, building, and finishing for an added-on room. Ouch. Now the second part of the equation: Are you sure you can recoup those costs when you sell?

Didn't think so. Stay with us—this book's for you.

We'll show you how to find or create space for your favorite activities. We'll show you how to reclaim your comfort zones by converting unused and poorly used space.

How to Use This Book

The pages of *IdeaWise Activity Spaces* are packed with images of interesting, attractive, efficient rooms. And although we hope you enjoy looking at them, they're more than pretty pictures: They're inspiration accompanied by descriptions, facts, and details meant to help you plan wisely.

Some of the rooms you see here will suit your sense of style, while others may not appeal to you at all. If you're serious about creating activity space, read it all—there's as much to learn in what you don't like as in what you do. Look at each photograph carefully and take notes. The details you gather are the seeds from which ideas will sprout.

The information in this book is divided into five activity areas: Home Offices; Specialty Work Spaces; Laundry & Mud Rooms; Arts, Crafts, and Hobbies; and Relaxation.

Within the chapters you'll find the following features:

DesignWise features hints and tips from professional designers and architects.

DollarWise describes money-saving ideas that can be adapted to your own plans and circumstances.

IdeaWise illustrates a clever do-it-yourself project for each topic.

One chapter also includes **Words to the Wise**, a glossary of terms that may not be familiar to you.

Another important feature of *IdeaWise Activity Spaces* is the Resource Guide on pages 130 to 139. The Resource Guide contains as much information as possible about most of the photographs in the book, including contact information for designers and manufacturers when available.

DesignWise

Robert Gerloff
Robert Gerloff Residential Architects
Minneapolis, MN

• Attach a small office to a detached garage so you can "leave" the office at the end of the day and "commute" home. This psychological distance makes work time more productive and home time more relaxing.

• Create a technology closet, a storage space behind a closed door where your laser printer, scanner, fax machine, modems, routers, hubs, and their whole tangle of cords can live out of sight. Connect to this network wirelessly, so your desk is clean and spare, and you can focus on work, not the clutter on your desk.

• Build a pin-up wall using cork or homosote bulletin board material, a wall where you can pin up projects like brochures or pamphlets to see how they look as a whole.

• Separate your office from your home acoustically. Install sound insulation between walls. Replace hollow core doors with solid core doors.

• Technology changes almost daily, so plan for constant change. Leave a 4" gap behind built-in desks for wires to fall. Place furniture or built-in cabinets 4" from the wall so cables and wires can snake behind them. Build in plenty of outlets and phone jacks below desk height in this 4" space.

DollarWise

CHALKBOARD PAINT

Chalkboard spray paint allows you to create a chalkboard on any wall or other flat surface (wood, metal, plastic, glass, paperboard, or hardboard) anywhere in your house.

You can buy the spray at your local home improvement store.

Simply mark off the area with painter's tape, then spray on three coats, allowing the chalkboard spray paint to dry between coats.

You will need to remove the painter's tape before the last coat dries to prevent lifting the ridges.

One can is enough for a 3' × 4' area; two cans will make a 4' × 6' chalkboard.

IdeaWise

PAPER-ON-A-ROLL

In this day of technology and carefully scheduled activities, it's nice to give a child a place to sit quietly and create. Attaching a large roll of butcher paper to an old table is a simple, inexpensive way to provide a continuous surface for paints, markers, and other media.

Attach brackets to a sturdy table, positioned to allow plenty of room for creativity. These brackets, as well as multi-colored paper, are available on-line as well as at art supply stores.

Words to the Wise

Fine Art: The study and creation of visual works of art.

Craft: An occupation or trade requiring manual dexterity or artistic skill.

Hobby: A pursuit outside of one's regular occupation, engaged in especially for pleasure.

CHAPTER 1

Home Offices

W hat are they?

"A home office" is a catchall term for any number of arrangements. It may refer to anything from a small desk in the kitchen corner to a spacious room filled with special furniture and equipment. A home office may be used for household tasks like paying bills and doing homework, or reserved for income-generating work. It may seat one person or be large enough to accommodate a good-sized conference table and comfy seating for clients. We'll cover a little bit of all of it in the coming pages.

Although we may not be able to agree on a definition of a home office, the majority of us (58 percent to be exact) want one for our very own, according to a recent survey of homeowners. For the 4,224,000 Americans who work at income-generating jobs exclusively from their homes, the home office is not a luxury—it's a necessity, and a serious one. For the home-based worker who lives with others—especially if those others are children—issues of privacy, noise control, family traffic, and protection of equipment become an interesting balancing act.

Mail Centers

If you're like most people, mail ends up carelessly tossed (or carefully stacked) on the dining room table, the kitchen island, or another spot where it doesn't belong. The problem, of course, is that it has no spot of its own. Mail does not "belong" anywhere in most homes because it's one of those overlooked and underestimated inconveniences of modern life. Ignore it though we may, it doesn't go away—in fact, every year there's more of it. Hence, we present the space we designate the "mail center."

The mail center is the daily repository and sorting site for mail. If there are young kids in the home, the site should also be spacious enough to accommodate the heap that they unload from their backpacks each day (homework, "art," announcements, and so on).

Mail management is a three-step process, each of which has its own space needs. To process incoming mail you need sorting space to separate the pieces that need attention—usually bills—from the junk destined for the recycling or trash bin. You also should have an assigned location—a cubby, a drawer, an "in box"—where unopened mail can sit undisturbed until you get a chance to process it. For outgoing mail, the mail center should have a reasonably clear, desk-like surface on which to write out bills, as well as a place to store stamps and envelopes. If your bill paying system is on a computer, you want space for that as well. Mail storage, the last process in mail management, refers to the file cabinet or other drawer where you store the bill-related paperwork you need to keep. In general, always shoot for the smallest possible distance between the place where incoming mail is sorted and outgoing mail is prepared and filed.

Open cubbies are the most convenient place to store unopened mail. Storing mail (specifically, bills) behind closed doors might be an invitation to forget about it.

Storage for a phone book within easy reach of the phone is a plus for any mail center.

Mail centers should include file drawers and closed cabinets to store paperwork. Lower drawers can be assigned to individual family members to keep homework and other belongings separate and accessible.

Pen, stamps, staplers, and other desk necessities should have a designated drawer or two so you can find them when you need them.

Mail centers are shared spaces; this increases the likelihood of chaos. In any activity space with multiple users, organized storage is indispensable. Tiny items like paper clips, staples, and lead refills have no choice but to scatter like seeds unless you're vigilant about using individual containers. If you don't have enough cubbies, consider adding small, decorative storage boxes.

Get as stylish as you need to be. A flashy galvanized metal in box works just as well as the dull plastic variety.

Any time you can add a bulletin board, chalkboard, dry erase board, or other place to post notes, do so.

The best place for your mail center is close to the outside door most frequently used by family members.

Convenience is key: Mail centers situated within current foot traffic patterns encourage family members to leave the mail in the right place. In this home, the small entrance between the kitchen and the side door works splendidly as a mail center.

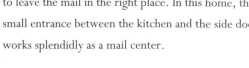

Locating the mail center in the kitchen is a great idea if you have the space. It's much easier to carve out space as part of a renovation than to try to squeeze it in as an afterthought. Corners—typically underused space—make excellent mail centers.

A small stretch of counter between cabinets
is another option for a bare-bones kitchen mail center.

Hallway Niches and Closets

Some of us have modest home office needs. We really don't need an extra bedroom or a "flex" or bonus room for home activities. In fact, most activities—including office work—can easily share space with other functions.

If you don't need a lot of physical space for your home office, we encourage you to think beyond the traditional notions of placement to the realities of your living space. Just about everyone can scare up a few extra square feet in an underused corner, an alcove, a nook, a window bay, under a staircase, a loft, or even in a closet.

Even small spaces can be successful offices if they're well lit, accessible, and furnished with an eye for both form and function.

Get off the beaten path: Finished attics provide out-of-the-way space if you prefer a little peace and quiet when you work. Kneewall nooks and crannies make sweet, secluded, hidden away home offices.

The landing at the top of the stairs becomes office space in these two homes. The trick is in sizing the activity areas so they don't interfere with the entrance to rooms or foot traffic to rooms. Doors need 36" of clearance in front of them.

Desks located on landings or in hallways need an outlet nearby for task lighting (and/or computers or other electronics). Extension cords are hazardous in these areas. If there's no outlet nearby and you don't know how to install one, hire an electrician.

This elegant desk on the loft overhang is surrounded by a child-proof balustrade. To maintain continuity with the room below and to retain a feeling of spaciousness, use the same materials for the ceiling and the underside of the loft. Providing phone access or an intercom in the loft helps users avoid running up and down the stairs more than necessary.

Wide, shallow closets can be easily converted to functional home office space when fitted with appropriate storage areas and work surfaces.

The opening in the half-wall gives a feeling of roominess and a nice sense of integration with the room. The office feels much bigger than it actually is.

These bi-fold doors, part of the original closet, keep the area out of view when it's not in use.

Spaces originally used as wet bars or walk-in closets are easy to convert into a simple basement home office. Spaces such as this may not have enough lighting for close work. No problem—just add lamps and other simple sources of task lighting.

If your office chairs have casters, carpeting is a drag—literally. These home-owners opted for wood floors in their office. If you choose carpeting, look for anti-static mats for medium pile, cut pile, and loop pile carpets.

Workstations keep desk contents neatly contained. Inexpensive versions are available pre-made or ready to assemble.

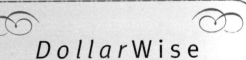

DollarWise

CHALKBOARD PAINT

Chalkboard spray paint allows you to create a chalkboard on any wall or other flat surface (wood, metal, plastic, glass, paperboard, or hardboard) anywhere in your house.

You can buy the spray at your local home improvement store.

Simply mark off the area with painter's tape, then spray on three coats, allowing the chalkboard spray paint to dry between coats.

You will need to remove the painter's tape before the last coat dries to prevent lifting the edges.

One can is enough for a 3' × 4' area; two cans will make a 4' × 6' chalkboard.

Some homeowners locate an office in a spare bedroom. This works when the office is for personal use only. Of course, you could never bring clients into this space.

It's satisfying to find a piece of furniture that fits a space exactly. Measure your rooms— especially nooks and alcoves— and keep the dimensions handy. You never know where you'll be when the perfect piece calls your name.

This homeowner relocated her desk to her bedroom because she works late at night and prefers being upstairs rather than on the main floor during the wee hours.

In smaller quarters, any space contains hidden possibilities. You can get infinitely creative with the space under stairways—building in small desk nooks, shelving, or storage space.

*Design*Wise

Robert Gerloff
Robert Gerloff Residential Architects
Minneapolis, MN

• Attach a small office to a detached garage so you can "leave" the office at the end of the day and "commute" home. This psychological distance makes work time more productive and home time more relaxing.

• Create a technology closet, a storage space behind a closed door where your laser printer, scanner, fax machine, modems, routers, hubs, and their whole tangle of cords can live out of sight. Connect to this network wirelessly, so your desk is clean and spare, and you can focus on work, not the clutter on your desk.

• Build a pin-up wall using cork or homosote bulletin board material, a wall where you can pin up projects like brochures or pamphlets to see how they look as a whole.

• Separate your office from your home acoustically. Install sound insulation between walls. Replace hollow core doors with solid core doors.

• Technology changes almost daily, so plan for constant change. Leave a 4" gap behind built-in desks for wires to fall. Place furniture or built-in cabinets 4" from the wall so cables and wires can snake behind them. Build in plenty of outlets and phone jacks below desk height in this 4" space.

In this shared space, Mom gets a chance to catch up on a few emails while her preschooler serves lunch to a bear. Barriers between work space and play areas don't need to be dramatic.

Shared Spaces

When you really think through the question of shared space vs. private space, you may be surprised at how few activities actually require private space. Most people prefer sitting within four to five feet of dining partners, watching television and listening to music with others, and sometimes—yes, sometimes—working in the vicinity of others. When it's not a matter of preference, it's often a matter of necessity.

Examine your family's habits. Every home has its own routines and rituals that determine where people tend to congregate. It's far easier to work with these behavioral patterns than to try to change them. If you look at them carefully, there's generally solid logic behind why habits become entrenched.

People under the age of ten have very little use for privacy and tend to fight it vigorously—they're positively driven to be underfoot. It's not entirely their fault —this familial closeness is a two-way street. Parents usually don't want great physical distance between themselves and young children. When distance is inevitable (as with the napping toddler upstairs), parents install audio and video monitors to, in effect, override the distance.

A home office may need to share space with a few dozen stuffed creatures or a train set. If this is your reality, embrace it. There are endless ways to make it work.

Something as simple as this drop leaf table creates an easy-to-remember boundary a child can learn to respect without feeling isolated from the working parent.

Bookcases add form and function to this activity space. Built-to-fit (BTF) shelving and cabinets are designed specifically for space that otherwise has no storage. It's the least expensive way to get efficient storage into your activity space.

In this home, the dining room doubles as a home office. This arrangement works easily as long as you control clutter enough that you can clear the table for meals.

In situations of reluctantly shared office space, locate the desk in a snug space that neither allows nor encourages a pileup of toys or other invitations to play. This will keep kiddie traffic to a minimum…unless, of course, the child provides his own transportation.

A full-sized, free-standing screen cuts down on visual distractions.

Homework Stations

Flexibility is key for homework spaces. What works at age 6 won't work at age 10, which, in turn, won't work at age14. Plan ahead.

Add small light fixtures above loft or bunk beds.

Built-to-fit (BTF) cabinets with both open and closed storage reduce clutter. The very top cabinets may be reserved for household storage since the kids can't reach them anyway.

If installing a homework station strains space in a child's bedroom, consider maximizing the bed footprint by buying a storage bed and getting rid of free-standing dressers.

Adjustable legs let a work table grow along with a child.

A loft bed with a desk, cabinets, and shelves directly below uses two small space strategies: 1) Spread up not out; 2) Organize loose papers in boxes on shelves. (You'll be glad for these boxes when it's time to dust.)

Modular, mobile furniture is about as kid-friendly as a piece of wood can get. If floor space is needed to build a fort or set up a racetrack, the wheeled unit glides away with a gentle shove.

Used to house toys now, these cubbies will be perfect for more mature playthings a few years from now—electronics, audio equipment, and so forth.

A brilliant example of flexible design, this modular desk evolves easily with a child's changing needs.

Short on space, long on creativity,
the homeowners bisected a wide, full-sized closet
to create a homework station on one side. A lou-
vered door slides to the right to reveal a homework
station, then back to the left to access clothing.

Computer Stations

When you make the transition from occupying a desk in a traditional workplace to setting up your own office at home, you discover intoxicating freedom and baffling responsibility, much of which will somehow involve your computer and its peripherals (and the lack of clever IT people to bail you out of every little e-glitch). Actually, glitches may be the least of your worries. More troublesome are the prospects of carpal tunnel syndrome, back stress, and eyestrain, much of which can be avoided by following a few simple, standard ergonomic procedures when setting up your new office space.

Plan for plenty of outlets near your computer. Outlets at desktop height will help you avoid a buildup of hard-to-reach and tangled cords behind your desk. As a precaution against blowing a circuit, you'll want to divide them into at least two separate circuits, if possible, and always use surge protectors for your computer and any sensitive electronics.

Choose an adjustable keyboard tray that also allows for a negative tilt (keyboard tilts away from you slightly) for optimum wrist comfort.

The ideal monitor placement allows 18" to 24" between your face and the screen (about arm's length). Sitting too close or too far can cause eyestrain. The top of the screen should be about even with your eyes.

Get an adjustable chair with lumbar support to protect your lower back from strain. When your feet are flat on the floor, your thighs should be roughly parallel to the floor.

Illuminate the work surface with under-cabinet lights as well as small lamps and other task lighting.

Off-white surfaces are easiest on the eyes. Working with white paper on a dark surface can cause eyestrain.

Most desks are 28 to 30" above the floor, however, the ideal keyboard height—the height at which you get the proper 90° angle—is 24 to 27" above the floor.

*Idea*Wise

Transform a plain table, desk or cabinet top into a fully equipped office with this box-style Secretary Topper.

Many catalogs offer products like this, but you could build one yourself with furniture grade plywood and lumber.

If you build a topper to fit on top of an existing piece of furniture, try to either match the wood type and finish or create enough contrast for it to appear deliberate. You could, for example, paint some portions and stain others to blend or match.

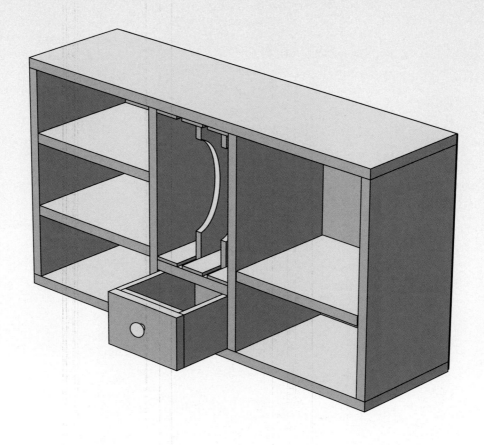

A separate entrance creates an atmosphere of professionalism and privacy for a home office.

It's impractical to use space above your head for storage. Instead, use high shelves to display collectibles or to showcase awards, diplomas, and other evidence of your professional credentials and expertise.

If your home office work includes visits from clients, you'll need a space where you're least likely to be interrupted by others in the household. Business visitors will feel more confident in your professionalism if you keep business as separate as possible from family life. In this home, the office space is separated from the family space by a half flight of stairs.

Office Lighting

Lighting is a personal issue. Some of us absolutely can't stand fluorescents; others feel anxious without natural light; some get headaches trying to read without bright lighting. So there's no "right" lighting design for a home office. We urge you to personalize your lighting to fit your preferences. That being said, there are certain benefits to natural light that deserve mention—especially if you have the option of adding a window or skylight to an otherwise windowless space.

Natural light appears to have a positive effect on mood for most people. On one end of the continuum are the people who suffer from seasonal affective disorder. This condition causes depression during the winter months due to the seasonal shortening of daylight hours. Fortunately, most of us don't get depressed due to the lack of natural light, but sunlight does seem to effect both children and adults in more subtle ways. Recent studies in the U.S., Canada and Sweden reveal that students attending day-lit schools outperformed students at non day-lit schools on standardized tests by 5 percent to 14 percent. They also were healthier, had more positive moods, had less dental decay, and grew better than students attending schools with average light.

Especially if you work long days or nights, an effective lighting plan makes an office more attractive and more comfortable. Consult a lighting designer, interior designer, or a good book on lighting design, and create a lighting plan that works for you.

Ideally, a combination of lighting sources
supports all of the activities your work requires.

To avoid screen glare,
keep monitors perpendicular to
windows and, if possible, tucked
into a slightly recessed area.

These cabinets have a halogen light strip
underneath. Under-cabinet strips can either be hard-
wired or plugged into existing electrical outlets.

Under-cabinet lighting becomes necessary when you mount cabinets directly above your desk. There are three types of under-cabinet fixtures: halogen, fluorescent, and compact fluorescent. Halogen bulbs, like common incandescent light bulbs, emit "warm" light, meaning they play up yellows and reds. Traditional fluorescent bulbs use less than half the electricity of other bulbs but produce "cool" light (green and blue hues), which many people find less pleasant than warm tones. The newer compact fluorescent (CFL) bulbs bring together the efficiency of the fluorescents with much warmer tones that closely replicate incandescent lighting.

Task lighting enhances work spaces.

Tabletop activities need about 120
watts of incandescent light or 35 watts
of fluorescent light for each 3 feet of work surface.

Task lights are never a bad idea in a home office—this is in addition to wall or ceiling mounted ambient lighting. For reading, you need 100 watts incandescent or 30 watts fluorescent lighting to prevent eyestrain.

CHAPTER 2

Specialty Work Spaces

In this chapter we'll look at the three most common specialty work areas found in homes today: workshops, music studios, and fitness centers. Specialty work spaces generally accommodate heavy or sensitive equipment that can't be moved and mustn't be disturbed. It also tends to require a little extra "proofing"—that is, sound-proofing, dust-proofing, or kid-proofing. Once they're set up, these spaces are more or less there to stay.

According to the National Association of Home Builders (NAHB), 25 percent of all remodeling projects are happening down in the basement. (Topping the list, predictably, are bathroom and kitchen remodeling—but that's a different book.) The cost of converting a basement into usable activity space is surprisingly reasonable. Starting from scratch, you could finish an average-sized basement (about 20 × 24") for less than $3,500 if you do all the work yourself. If you have all the work done by professionals, the cost should come to between $9,000 to $9,500.

If you don't have a basement or it's already in use, consider the garage. The beauty of garages is that they're relatively easy and inexpensive to convert to activity space. Whether you're working with an attached or detached garage, you've already paid for the excavation, foundation, framing, and closing in of the space. All that's left: wiring, heating, cooling, and floor covering.

Workshops

Among do-it-yourselfers, perhaps the single space most fervently wished for is a workshop. Not just any workshop—a clean, well-organized, well-lit, well-equipped space.

These 4-ft. fluorescent "shop lights" can be very inexpensive—as low as $10 each—but the low-end fixtures have low-quality ballasts that make an irritating buzzing sound. They also take longer to warm up in cold temperatures. Consider investing in higher quality fixtures with industrial ballasts. They're quieter, warm up more quickly, and last longer.

Pegboard remains the least expensive, easiest way to organize and store hand tools. Look for hooks with plastic clips—they keep the hooks from pulling loose each time you grab a tool.

Plan on one outlet about every six feet. If you must use extension cords, use heavy-grade extension cords in the shortest length possible.

Leave room for a garbage can to collect small pieces of scrap lumber and cutoffs as you work.

Figure you'll need about one third of your workshop space for permanent storage, stationary tools, and fixtures. Everything else falls into two categories: light and heavy. Mount lighter things on the walls and ceilings. Put heavy items on wheels.

Most garages offer enough space for a well-planned workshop.
In this home, a simple combination of storage cabinets framing a pegboard wall

provides enough work and storage space for household projects.

Never underestimate the advantage of ample storage. Workshops generally require several types of storage, open as well as closed. Cabinets and drawers are ideal for storing blades, bits, smaller shop tools, and other loose articles. Consider drawers with locks if there are small children in your home. Narrow, wall-mounted shelves are good for storing spare lumber and finishing materials.

Workshop phones are more than a convenience— they're safety features. Other safety must-haves: A first-aid kit and a fire extinguisher.

Workshops require two circuits: one for lighting, the other for electrical outlets. Consider installing a third dedicated circuit if you're running an air conditioner or large electric heater in your shop. Another option is a smaller subpanel of additional circuit breakers—this option allows you to switch circuits on and off without having to access the main panel. If you lack experience, consult a licensed electrician before starting any electrical work.

Air quality is important in workshops.

Air quality needs to be a priority in workshops. Vapors from stains, varnishes, and other finishing products are not just unpleasant, they're toxic. To avoid overexposure, you need fresh air. Keep windows and doorways open, set up portable fans to create cross-breezes, and use ceiling fans to circulate air. Chronic, long-term exposure to solvents may have adverse effects on the liver, heart, and reproductive systems. It also can cause permanent brain and nervous system damage. If your workshop has no windows, install them. Access fresh air!

Dust collection systems remove sawdust from the air. At the very minimum you need a shop vac permanently stationed in your workshop. If your workshop includes a table saw, sanders, planers, or other prolific dust producers, you may want to invest in a dedicated dust collector to capture sawdust and wood debris right at the source. Disposable respirators and those with replaceable filters help keep wood dust out of your lungs.

Traditional Workbenches

Workbenches come in a variety of sizes and styles,
but they basically fit into one of three categories: traditional benches,
utility benches, and portable benches. Traditional benches have extra-
thick surfaces and sturdy wooden legs that keep the bench stationary and
absorb the vibrations of hammering. The top surface is usually hard
maple, beech, or other hardwood laminate. Traditional benches are free-
standing units, generally about 2 feet wide and 4 to 6 feet long. They
also generally come with at least one end vise and bench dogs for holding
work pieces securely. Expect to pay about $500 for a good workbench.

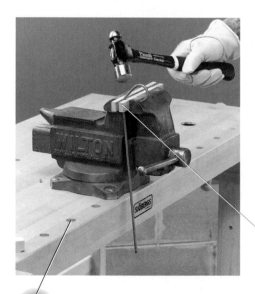

*Line vise jaws with wood to keep metal
jaws from marring soft wood pieces.*

*Bench dogs hold work
pieces securely in place.*

*Idea*Wise

If you can't justify shelling out half a grand for a workbench, you can make your own for less than $100. Use double 2X4s to make the legs, and design the bench with a sturdy framework of 2X4s under the top surface. For the top, use medium-density fiberboard (MDF). MDF is a very dense material with a flat, smooth surface that won't splinter. It's rugged and durable, though the edges might begin to show wear and tear after a while. To protect the edges, trim them out in hardwood. You can add an open shelf or closed cabinets below. Keep the width under 3 feet and the length less than 8 feet. If you need a mobile workbench, buy heavy-duty casters rated for at least 100 pounds each. Larger diameter wheels make the bench easier to maneuver. Two of the four casters must have brakes so the bench doesn't roll when in use.

With direct-vent heaters, the flue gas vent is either installed through the wall and routed directly to the outside or routed outside via the ceiling. Sealed combustion heaters are the safest type of direct-vent heaters, as they feature a sealed glass cover that keeps room air from being combusted. These heaters burn outdoor air only and are less likely to back-draft.

If your workshop is located in an attached garage, your best bet is to extend the heating and cooling system from the house into the converted workshop. It's not a time-consuming nor necessarily expensive project to undertake, yet it's best to get professional advice if you've never worked with heating/cooling systems before.

If extending the system isn't possible, there are a couple other ways to bring heat into the workshop. Woodstoves are energy-efficient options, and they are reasonably priced; however, they require a metal or masonry chimney and need regular maintenance to function safely and efficiently.

Direct vent space heaters can be an excellent heating option for garage workshops—if you're smart and safe about your choice of heater. Vented units must be permanently located next to an outside wall. You'll need to have your vented space heater professionally inspected once a year to minimize risk of carbon monoxide poisoning through blocked or damaged vents. Unvented combustion heaters are too risky for indoor workshops. Instead of venting combustion byproducts outside, they are vented into the room. This poses indoor air quality issues. Do not use them to heat your workshop.

*Design*Wise

Chris Marshall

Author and
Woodworking Expert

WORKSHOP ORGANIZATION

• With shop lighting, the goal is to minimize shadows and have focused light where it matters most. Fluorescent fixtures provide energy-efficient ceiling lighting, but you'll also want several bulb-style task lights: one over the bench and others wherever you are doing intricate work.

• Large machinery, cabinets, and even your workbench are easier to store and move around if you mount them on four sturdy casters. Buy two that swivel and two that don't. Choose the swiveling casters with locks so your machines and fixtures will stay put where you want them.

• Every good workshop needs a good workbench—but you don't have to spend a fortune on one. See the IdeaWise on the previous page for an example of an inexpensive workbench.

• Just say no to clutter: Toss scraps shorter than a foot in length; dispose of cans of paint or finish older than a year or two; sell or give away tools you don't actually use.

Music Studios

Home recording studios range from the simple (under $1,000) to the sublime (professional quality), but they all require at least a modicum of soundproofing. Basements become the natural choice for music studios because they're somewhat removed from the noise of the rest of the house for recording purposes; they also help keep the music being played from disturbing the peace in the rest of the house.

This studio belongs to a sound recording professional who works from home. This elaborate setup illustrates how versatile a home office can be. Be willing to dream big and invest in elements that will give you the highest return on your money.

For professional quality recording, sound isolation is a must. Glass-paneled doors let you see into the booth while recording is in session.

Although today's music incorporates technology more than ever, recording and mixing sound can be done in an office or bedroom. Plenty of storage and separate work areas keep a music studio organized and productive.

Music is integrated into the everyday life of this family—the piano and microphone take center stage. When adding a piano, make sure the floor is well supported and the floor covering durable. Place furniture coasters under the piano legs to evenly distribute the weight and protect the floor covering.

When planning the arrangement of audio equipment, provide enough properly placed outlets to power the equipment without tangles of extension cords.

Draperies, rugs, and/or
carpet absorb vibrations
and reduce transmission of sound
to other parts of the house.

Fitness Centers

In the last three years, sales of home gym equipment have risen 19 percent to an annual $4.67 billion according to the National Sporting Goods Association, the industry's largest retail trade association. And it's not only spring chickens going for the burn: Treadmills, which are by far the most frequently purchased gym item, are being snapped up at an astonishing rate by 45- to 64-year-olds. That group alone accounts for 44 percent of treadmill sales. Moral of this story: Getting fit is fab at any age.

If you're extremely motivated, you need nothing more than a jump rope, resistance bands, an exercise mat, and a couple hand weights to achieve the streamlined form you desire. For the rest of us, there are treadmills, ellipticals, stationary bikes, and those seriously complex multi-station gyms.

No matter what equipment or activity you prefer, it's easier and more fun to work out in a comfortable, well-lit, well-organized space.

Free weight setups need about 20 to 50 square feet and are the most economical alternative in strength training. Plan on about 50 cents per pound for cast-iron weights (around 80 cents to $1 a pound for vinyl or neoprene weights). Benches are an additional $60 to $250.

Natural light makes your home fitness center far more inviting than it would be with only artificial lighting.

Ceiling fans keep the air moving—the breeze just might keep you moving, too. Operable windows and good ventilation are a must in fitness centers.

Blinds provide privacy without sacrificing air flow, an important consideration.

Treadmills run anywhere from $300 to $4,000. Of course, quality varies in proportion to cost. The American College of Sports Medicine recommends spending no less than $2,000 on a treadmill if you're a runner (in which case, look for 2.0-horsepower or higher) and no less than $1,000 if you're a walker (requiring only 1.5-horsepower.) Set aside 30 square feet of floor space for your treadmill unless you're buying one that folds up. Whether looking at used or new machines, here's a good way to make sure you're getting a sound machine: Stomp both feet on the belt while the motor is running. If you hear any grinding sounds or groaning, you're stomping on an inferior machine. Keep looking.

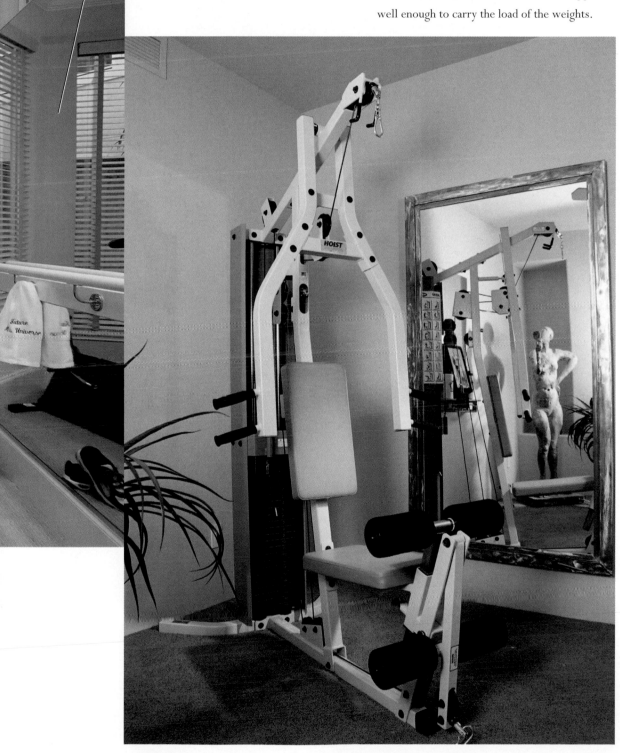

If it's helpful, install a mirror on one wall. If it's depressing, skip it.

If you're looking at strength training equipment, you'll need about 35 square feet of space for a single station setup and somewhere between 50 to 500 square feet for a multi-station model. If your fitness center is not in the basement, make sure the floor is supported well enough to carry the load of the weights.

CHAPTER 3

Laundry and Mud Rooms

In a recent survey, the National Association of Home Builders (NAHB) asked respondents what types of rooms they would want in their home for luxury and convenience. Ninety-two percent wanted a laundry room.

It's pretty much a given that we all want space in which to do laundry. Now—where should it be? To answer that question, look at existing habits. Suppose you spend most waking hours on the main floor. Though a second floor laundry near the bedrooms would save you the trip upstairs with clean laundry, it ultimately makes extra work if you have to run upstairs each time you switch loads. For this reason, laundry rooms adjacent to kitchens are popular. The beauty of this arrangement is that laundry rooms can double as mud rooms if located near the back door. Also, it's efficient (and therefore economical) to install laundry facilities near an existing plumbing stack.

How much space you need depends on the size and habits of your family. Smaller households that generate a few loads a week may prefer a laundry space located off a hallway or in an alcove. On the other hand, larger families or families with young children typically appreciate larger laundry areas with folding counters and plenty of storage space.

Appliances

When it comes to choosing appliances for your laundry room, it's hard to go wrong. After all, any good quality washer will get your clothes clean, and any good quality dryer will dry them. The differences between models and types are mostly a matter of capacity, energy and water efficiency, style, and price.

If you plan to place the washer and dryer under a counter, choose units with controls on the front panel.

Make sure you have enough clearance for the doors to open and plenty of room to transfer laundry from the washer to the dryer.

Front-loading washers typically cost more than top loaders to purchase, but they cost less to operate because they use less water and energy. Fast spin speeds remove water efficiently, which reduces drying time and energy consumption. (A front loader saves the average family about $90 a year.)

Many experts believe that front-loading machines, which don't have agitators, are gentler to clothing than top loaders. Standard capacity for front-loading washers is 12 to 20 pounds—about 16 pairs of jeans or 12 queen-size sheets.

Placing the appliances on an outside wall makes it easy to vent the dryer, an absolute necessity.

Top-loading machines are less expensive to buy but slightly more expensive to run than front-loading machines because they use more water and electricity. Although they have traditionally used agitators, new technology has reduced the amount of stress top loaders place on fibers. In many models, new designs have expanded capacity as well. (Standard capacity for a top-loading washer is 12 to 16 pounds per load, the equivalent of 9 to 12 pairs of jeans.)

The major decision point for dryers is whether to choose gas or electric power. Gas dryers cost slightly more to purchase but less to operate, particularly because they dry clothing quicker. Every dryer—gas or electric—must be vented to the outside.

Laundry Rooms

A room dedicated to laundry is the number one luxury requested by prospective home buyers these days. And no wonder! The average family does eight to ten loads of laundry every week, according to a survey sponsored by the Whirlpool Corporation.

Just like everything else in home design, laundry room trends come and go over time. And the great debate about laundry rooms these days is placement—should it be in the basement, near the garage or kitchen, or close to the bedrooms? The answer depends on the size and lifestyle of your family, and only you know what works best for your circumstances. But no matter where it's located, an efficient laundry room has certain features such as the ones shown on the next few pages.

Semi-gloss or high-gloss paints are more resistant to water and easier to keep clean and bright than flat or eggshell. If you use wallpaper, choose one labeled scrubbable, not just washable. It will stand up better to rugged use.

Flooring should be water resistant and easy to clean. Vinyl, linoleum, laminate, and tile are good options.

In small laundry rooms, every inch of space has to be put to good use. Here, cabinets and countertops offer storage and a folding surface. A window and mirror brighten the small space, which is carefully kept free of clutter to make laundry chores more pleasant.

Decant detergents and fabric softeners from unattractive large boxes and plastic jugs into more attractive containers.

Use separate baskets for freshly laundered clothing, linen, and towels headed for separate destinations.

If you have the space for it, a table is an affordable luxury.

In many homes, the laundry room is morphing into a multi-purpose room, combining space for household chores with space for hobbies and homework of all sorts.

This "drying cabinet" allows you to air dry clothing relatively quickly. Clothing is dried in a few hours instead of a few days.

Keep supplies organized according to task. Anything you regularly need for ironing should be within easy reach of the iron.

Flip-down ironing boards are fabulous space savers.

A combination of open and closed storage is ideal for the laundry room. Keep open cubbies organized and attractive by storing frequently used small supplies in baskets or bins: Place sewing materials in one, laundry specialty products in another, and sponges in a third.

The island makes an ideal center for folding clothes, wrapping gifts, and other large projects.

Devote a bit of storage space for books and toys that will amuse small children or grandchildren who have come to help you in the laundry room.

Washing and drying the laundry is only half the battle. It still needs to get put away—a sticking point for many families. Rather than fight the problem, plan for it. Add plenty of open storage, designate a shelf or basket for each family member, and neatly stack clean clothes there. That way, cabinets and counters remain tidy, even when someone "forgets" to put away their laundry. Again.

Alcove Laundry

If your laundry room is not actually a room, but a small hallway niche or an alcove off a larger room, the space saving principle comes into effect: Spread up like here, not out. Epoxy-coated wire shelving systems can be configured in any arrangement you need as all the components are sold separately.

Wherever possible, run shelves all the way to the ceiling. Put frequently used items within reach and use the remaining space for specialty items.

A bar hanging below a high shelf provides a place for clothes to line dry.

Rolling bins simplify laundry tasks. Label each bin and encourage family members to pre-sort whites, colors, and delicates.

In small spaces, the best solutions often are simple and inexpensive. Here, basic brackets and melamine boards provide shelves, and a standard closet rod provides a place to line dry delicate pieces.

The ultimate response to the "go up, not out" philosophy, a stacked washer and dryer leaves enough room in this closet for a much needed shelving system.

Mud Rooms

Though not yet a mainstay in American housing, mud rooms are gaining popularity—and for good reason. Usually located directly inside a rear entry to the house, the mud room, as its name implies, acts as the buffer between outdoor dirt and grime and the inside of your home. This is where householders remove wet or muddy shoes and outerwear before continuing inside. Though it doesn't have to be a large area, ideally, the mud room should offer hooks or pegs for jackets and dog leashes, a bench where people can sit to remove or put on boots, an umbrella stand, mats on the floor, and shelving or cubbies for hats, gloves, helmets, bats, balls, or whatever else you don't want in the house.

Traditional mud rooms are built to be hosed down, so walls are tiled instead of wallpapered or painted. If you're not prepared to go that far, choose scrubbable, durable wall covering or paint.

*Idea*Wise

MAKE YOUR OWN DUCKBOARD

Duckboards are mats made of slatted wood meant to allow snowy or wet boots to drain until dry. The underside has rubber footings meant to keep the duckboard from slipping on the floor. Plastic trays can be slid into the 3" high space below the duckboards to catch shoe drippings.

Beech or pine is a good choice for the wood.

Dimensions should be approximately 26" × 15".

Lightly oil with boiled linseed oil or sunflower oil.

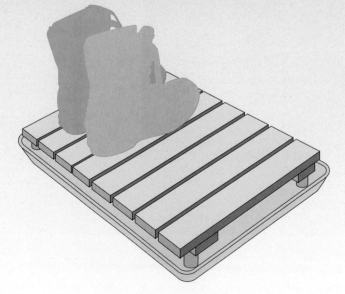

Choose flooring that can hold up under water, grime, and street salt or sand. Your best bets are vinyl, brick, concrete, natural slate, or tile. Choose flooring with a high coefficient of friction and load up on floor mats to keep the floors from becoming slippery when wet.

Hooks should be plentiful and at various heights so children can reach them, too.

A mud room should include a place to sit down while putting on or removing boots. A built-in open bench with shoe storage below is ideal.

Wicker baskets minimize musty odors by promoting air flow.

Hooks take care of everything from head scarves to handbags.

In areas with lots of wet or wintry weather, built-in duckboard makes the best shelving for boots and shoes.

If your home lacks a designated mud room (and most homes do), there are other ways to set up an area near an entrance that can provide many of the same functions. Here, cubbies, hooks, and a padded bench built onto the wall separating the entrance from the dining room serve as a compact mud room.

A narrow niche in a back hallway serves as the mud room area, providing a bench for removing shoes, open storage, and a few pegs for jackets and the dog leash.

Any wall near the rear entry of your home can be transformed into mudroom function. Home-improvement stores, catalogs, and websites provide every possible configuration for wall-mounted shelving and cubbies.

*Design*Wise

Susan Nackers Ludwig

Rehkamp Larson Architects, Inc. Minneapolis, MN

LAUNDRY

• Create under-counter shelves for laundry baskets or pull-out bins. It's a great place to store clothes waiting to be washed or put away.

• Allow for task lighting. Place a light fixture above the washer and dryer, another above a sink, and one near the folding area.

• Place a hanging rod above a sink. It's a perfect place to let your clothes drip dry without getting the floor wet.

MUD ROOM

• Give each person their own storage area in the mud room. It could be a basket, cubby space, or locker. This avoids misplaced items like hats and mittens in the winter and is a great place to put a purse or backpack.

• More efficient storage can make up for a lack of floor space. Allow storage to go all the way to the ceiling. You can put your out-of-season gear in the hard-to-reach areas.

• Add a mirror to the mud room. You can see what you look like before you leave, and it can make the space feel larger.

• Select flooring with a pattern or texture instead of a solid color. Solid surfaces tend to show more dirt and traffic wear.

In this home, a 6-foot stretch of wall

substitutes for a traditional mud room. Wire shelving systems, sold as separate components, allow customization to suit the space.

You don't need a huge bench for your mud room. A one-person stool is sufficient for many smaller mud room spaces.

Natural light is always welcome in a mud room or laundry. Here, a shelf placed beneath the window creates a pleasant spot for folding laundry.

Mud rooms and laundry rooms are natural companions.

If you have enough space, an area like this is a great place to store sporting gear—especially sports uniforms, which seem perpetually dirty. If they're stored in the laundry room, there's a much better chance they'll get washed in time for the next big game.

A shower is a wonderful amenity.

Where space and budget permit, a shower is a wonderful amenity in a mud room. A hand-held shower hose or sprayer makes washing the dog a more pleasant experience for pooch and person alike. And if your work or hobby leaves you covered in grime at the end of a day, a mud room shower lets you leave all traces of it beyond your living space.

The mud room is an ideal location for an indoor kennel like this. The dog door cut into the exterior wall allows this pampered pet to let himself in and out at will. With plexiglass on both doors, he always has a view to the outside—and inside—world.

An elogated faucet allows easy access for filling buckets and cleaning large-scale projects.

A drying rack close to the tub makes the task at hand convenient and tidy.

A utility floor sink is an affordable alternative to a full-sized shower. This one includes duckboards that can be lowered into place as needed.

Durable tile is the perfect surface for messy cleanups.

CHAPTER 4

Arts, Crafts and *Hobbies*

B etween email, e-learning, e-commerce, e-books, and eBay, it would seem keyboard dexterity now ranks higher than the opposable thumb. Welcome to the virtual age. Fortunately, the innate value of handiwork is not lost on modern humans. As we use our hands less to work, clean, and cook, our collective urge to create with our hands grows stronger.

Research recently released by the Hobby Industry Association shows that 58 percent of us indulge in some form or art, craft, or hobby at home, and this number creeps up each year.

The craft and hobby industry now accounts for over $25 billion in annual sales in the U.S. The five most popular crafts, in order of popularity, are cross-stitch, home decor painting, scrapbooking and memory crafts, floral arranging, and crocheting.

The typical crafter or hobbyist spends 7.5 hours per week working in their home on various projects. Over the course of a year this adds up to close to 400 hours! Not surprisingly, many people are interested in making the space devoted to their crafts and hobbies as comfortable, inviting, organized, and efficient as possible.

Cross-stitching, crocheting, and other needlecrafts are compact, portable, and don't generally take up much space, so they aren't discussed in this chapter. We do, however, address space for painting, sewing, scrapbooking, and a handful of hobbies with special space requirements: indoor gardening, wine collecting, and other collections.

Among artists there's little agreement on how to define "art" as distinct from "craft," and we won't enter that rhetorical quagmire here. For our purposes, we'll assign painting, sculpture, and ceramics to the art section as they have somewhat different activity space requirements.

Northern light is ideal for drafting tables and easels because it provides consistent, even sunlight. If you can install only one window or skylight, go for northern exposure.

The quietness and remoteness of an attic holds a certain amount of creative allure. Building codes usually require that a "habitable room" have at least 70 square feet of floor space. Any attic area with a ceiling height under 5 feet would not be counted toward the 70 square feet.

Garage studios for painting, music record-ing, and ceramic work are becoming more popular all the time. One reason is that many garages are now built with bonus room or loft space atop. Cement floors and bare bones walls are perfect surfaces for the stains, splatters, and spills that accompany any serious artwork.

Ventilation is essential because clay and glaze dust can be hard on lungs. Open air is fabulous, but you'll still need a respirator or dust mask for mixing clay.

Clay work is extremely messy, so the ideal pottery space has walls and floors that can handle wet splatters and be hosed down easily, like the cement floor you see here.

A room of one's own…

A separate room isn't mandatory for an artist, of course, but designated space is. If all supplies and projects have to be cleared away at the end of every session, what should be a pleasure becomes an exercise in aggravation, and the urge to create has to be confined to blocks of time large enough to gather and replace all the supplies.

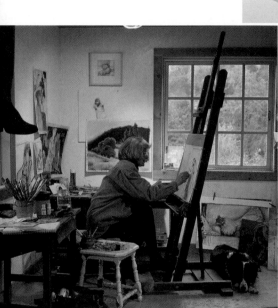

Surprisingly, windows aren't always the best light source for art studios. The ideal is high windows with northern exposure. Other orientations sometimes admit too much or fragmented light, which casts shadows. If your windows are less than ideal, cover them with thin, translucent roller shades or paper to mute light, then add task lighting.

Art studio basics include neutral walls and floors, good ventilation, and a door that closes. Why a door, you ask? As the saying goes, creative minds are rarely tidy, and it's handy to close the door on the mess. Plus, as any artist can tell you, it's easier to take risks with your work without comments from well-meaning loved ones. If your studio space doesn't have a door, buy a folding screen or hang curtains.

Decorative painting is popular in many forms. *Rosemaling*, a centuries-old art form refers to the decorative painting style you see in this studio. Important features for a decorative painting studio include "curing" shelves (for painted objects that might take up to ten days to dry), and closets or cabinets in which to store assorted paints, brushes, and cleaners.

Sewing & Quilting

Space to spread out, room to leave projects-in-progress and return to find them just as you left them, places to store all your tools and treasures—these are the dreams of sewers and quilters. Lots of storage, comfortable work surfaces, and good lighting are the foundations of good sewing rooms.

Abundant light, space, storage, and work surfaces make this sewing room a pleasant, efficient place to work and play.

Full-spectrum light bulbs produce the color-correct light that's essential when designing with fabric.

"So much fabric, so little space," bemoan fabric collectors, for whom storage is always at a premium. Here, a corner closet stores yard goods and notions.

Computer software helps sewers generate quilt designs, create and store patterns, and produce elaborate machine embroidery motifs.

Bi-fold doors shield fabrics from potentially damaging sunlight.

Flexible task lights reduce eyestrain.

Wall-mounted spool racks keep thread organized and accessible.

A good sewing chair has back support, is height adjustable, and has casters for mobility.

Reserve the small drawer closest to you for seam rippers, scissors, tape measures, and other small, often used items.

*Idea*Wise

MAKE YOUR OWN SEWING STATION:

Buy a 5-foot section of kitchen countertop from your local home improvement store. (You should be able to buy a remnant section for about $20.) Center the countertop on top of two metal file cabinets. Place your cutting mat on half the countertop and cover the other half with batting. Cover the batting with silver ironing cloth for pressing tasks.

The best height for a cutting table depends on the height of the user, of course, but most people are comfortable working at tables between 36" and 40" high.

Positioning an ironing board next to the sewing machine at a height that can be reached while seated eliminates the constant up-and-down of construction pressing. L-, T-, and U-shaped spaces work better than straight-line workspaces.

Well-organized, simple pieces create an efficient working arrangement for this quilter. The cutting center includes the cutting table, lighting, and storage for tools and supplies.

Every year there are more and more spectacular task lamps on the market. For sewing, quilting, and crafting, "daylight simulation" bulbs provide perfect color matching. These bulbs give off little heat, are energy saving, and provide even light distribution. To further reduce eyestrain, consider a lamp with a built-in magnifying lens for detailed work.

Dollar Wise

For people who attend sewing classes or get together with friends to sew or quilt, small cutting mats are terrific. The problem is, the mats often get rolled or wrinkled in transit. There's no reason to throw away a wrinkled mat—you can straighten it out easily. Heat your oven to 250 degrees for 10 minutes, then turn it off. Place the cutting mat on an upside-down cookie sheet in the heated oven. It will straighten itself out beautifully in just a minute or so. (Make sure the oven is off before you place the cookie sheet inside!)

Other Crafts

Some crafts involve assembling materials from several sources. Scrapbooking, rubber stamping, card crafting, framing, and floral arranging fall into this category. Whether you have only a small corner in a shared space for crafting or an entire room, your activity space will quickly become clogged and unusable if you don't put some thought into its design.

Plan on earmarking about 50 percent of your craft space for storage.

A mixture of ambient lighting and task lights work best for crafting spaces.

Comfortable, low-armed chairs are great places to sit for hand-finishing tasks.

Call on your creative muses to assemble a crafting area that inspires you. Built-in cabinets, antique furniture, and any other storage facilities that please you are fair game.

When it comes to supplies, out-of-sight can easily become out-of-mind. Clear storage boxes provide reminders of exactly what you have on hand.

Shelves line the walls surrounding this work surface, creating storage space for the thousands of shells, beads, buttons, and stones this crafter has collected.

Customize the space to the activity.

Ventilation is especially important in rooms used for crafts that include volatile compounds and other smelly substances, such as the glues and paints used in model making. An operating window or two is best, but fans may be necessary in some cases.

Building display space into work centers gives you places to show off your accomplishments.

*Design*Wise

Rosemary McMonigal, AIA

McMonigal Architects
Minneapolis, MN
612-331-1244

WINE CELLAR INSULATION

• To maintain proper humidity and temperature levels in your wine cellar, create a vapor barrier separation. Insulate the space between studs with batting, then attach sheets of 5 mil. polyethlyene over the studwalls and seal the joints. You could also use rigid insulation behind studs with an open study cavity.

SEWING ROOM SAVVY

• Sewing projects produce clutter, so set up space where you can manage clutter easily. If you don't have a separate room for sewing, a shared space will work fine as long as it's away from the main traffic in your home.

• Natural light is an important factor in a fully functional sewing room. Natural lighting reveals the true color balance of the materials you're working with. Even "color corrected" artificial lighting isn't the same. The natural light from windows is also essential to give your eyes a break from the strain of stitching work. Finally, you will appreciate the ventilation a window affords.

INDOOR GARDENING

• Indoor gardening and seeding requires two distinct spaces. You need a permanent storage area to store fertilizers, potting soils, seedling containers and other supplies, and a second space with a sink and counter for re-potting and seeding. This might be the laundry room, kitchen, or utility area.

• If you want to start seedlings in a space without natural light, set up seedling racks (fixtures that slide up and down to adjust to plant or flower height) beneath adjustable grow lights .

• Use a "heat mat" if your seeding space is cool. Seedling heat mats are water resistant electric heating pads made to fit below all standard growing flats and seedling trays. They elevate the seeding medium 10 to 12 degrees above room temperature for stronger roots and quicker germination.

Wine Cellars

The modern home-based "wine cellar" no longer implies an elaborate cellar or even a specific room. Today, everything from simple racks to refrigerated storage units can be found on any or every level of a home.

Cooled storage maintains an even coolness (about 55° F) and a humidity level between 50 to 70 percent, the ideal conditions for storing wine.

A traditional below-grade cellar

meets the temperature and humidity requirements for storing wine without any cooling equipment because the natural ground temperature is about 55°F. If your wine storage space doesn't meet these conditions, you can create them by installing a cooling system in a sealed off room. Slate, tile, marble, or vinyl are fine for flooring, but never use carpet—it will create mold and mildew in cool, damp conditions.

Standard wine racks should be made of soft wood that won't rot in cool, humid conditions. Redwood or mahogany are the best choices.

Wine cellars with built-in cooling units

have to be sealed off from the rest of the house to contain the cool air. Use only well-sealed, exterior grade (1¾") doors with weather stripping on all four sides of the doorjamb and a bottom sweep to prevent air leakage. Although solid core doors are used most often, glass doors—like the one seen here—are suitable as long as they're constructed with at least double-glazed, double-tempered glass.

Indoor Gardening

In many areas, winter lacks color. Leaves disappear, leaving spindly branches. Snow blankets dormant grass. As the landscape fades to shades of white, gray, and black, we respond with a craving for color. This is the point at which our houseplants take on extra importance.

Not only do they bolster our spirits, plants actually make our indoor environment a shade healthier by removing carbon dioxide from the air and releasing oxygen and small amounts of humidity.

For the indoor gardener, the benefits of houseplants outweigh any inconvenience of repotting, pruning, and seeding. It's dirty business, but you don't need a lot of space. A designated space, no matter how small, is delightful.

Indoor gardening space needs as much counter space as you can muster, both for work and for storage of containers and other supplies.

A retired trellis is called back to work as pegboard for a temporary outdoor potting station.

Any weatherized or weather-beaten table works well outdoors.

During the warm summer months, transfer your potting equipment outdoors and create a workstation for your outdoor garden.

Greenhouses

Though we tend to associate the word with large, independent structures, a greenhouse is any heated structure—from a mere window bay to an entire room—that traps sunlight and moisture. Plants inside a greenhouse thrive during times when the same plants would go dormant or die outdoors. Greenhouses are useful in all climate zones.

Lean-to greenhouses are far less expensive to build than freestanding greenhouses because they use an existing structure for one or more sides. They also have the advantage of close proximity to available electricity, water, and heat.

A window green-house, also called a garden window, is the most compact and least expensive way to provide greenhouse benefits to indoor plants. These windows project from the wall 16 to 24" and usually have side or front opening windows for ventilation. Replacing a regular window with a prefabricated greenhouse window is a fairly simple project.

Who loves a garden loves a greenhouse too.
Unconscious of a less propitious clime,
There blooms exotic beauty, warm and snug,
While the winds whistle, and the snows descend.

—William Cowper (1731-1800)

Collections & Displays

Collecting is an art form that deserves some respect. Were it not for myriad patient, dedicated, detail-oriented individuals who devote years to amassing collections, there would be no museums, antiques, archives, or libraries. Even if your collection will never be seen outside your home, it still deserves safe storage and dignified display.

Collections can anchor a
room's decor as does this collection
of vintage textiles.

Larger collectibles—woven blankets
and baskets in this case—bring opportunities
for creative and charming display solutions.

Shelf units are heavy, and must be hung from or connected to wall studs at several locations.

Display cabinets don't have to be expensive or elaborate. Here, built-to-fit, compartmentalized shelves provide display space for a collection of handblown glass.

In this family's seaside home, when seashell collecting was a casual pursuit—not necessarily a valued activity—shells were scattered throughout the house. Now that the homeowners have designated this cabinet as a display area, years' worth of shells remain unbroken and preserved.

CHAPTER 5

Relaxation

With each generation, Americans gain new technology to help take the edge off. Machines allow us to wash, cook, and mow the lawn with ever fewer steps. We open the garage, do our banking, and order pizza from the front seat of our car. We have personal portable stereos channeling soothing sounds directly to our eardrums 24/7.

With so many stress-relieving amenities, why are we so uptight? An alarming 15 to 33 percent of American adults suffer from hypertension, putting us at greater risk for heart attacks and strokes than ever before.

Ironically, despite the scads of money we spend on luxury, convenience, and hobby pursuits, we have not learned to relax. We cram our daily schedules—weekends, too—and promise to make up for all the rushing and stress during our annual vacation. Problem is, by the time we get those two weeks off (if we take them) our arteries are that much harder, thanks to the relentless pace.

Relaxation can't be banked like vacation hours, physiologically speaking. Putting it off is like saying you won't eat this month, but you'll make up for it later. We need to indulge in a small amount of relaxation every day to recharge and repair our bodies and minds. Most of us really need no more than about 20 minutes a day. There are as many ways to relax as there are people reading this book. They're all good as long as they leave you feeling calmer and more capable. Relaxation is an activity that earns its own space daily.

For most of us, our moments of relaxation take place somewhere in our homes. In this chapter we'll explore interior spaces devoted to relaxation.

Family Rooms

A family room with south or west facing windows glows with natural light in the afternoon.

The ratio 3:5 describes the proportion—or the relationship—between the heights of the fireplace and the bookcases that surround it. The proportion 3 to 5 is famous in design circles. It's called the Golden Mean, and it's been used extensively in Western architecture and art for millennia and is thought to have an intrinsically pleasing, calming effect on the human psyche.

The fireplace is the focal point of this room. If you were to imagine a dividing line from the ridge straight down through the fireplace, the left and right sides of the photo would be basically mirror images of one another. This is the design principle of symmetry.

The success of any design depends upon how well the creation fulfills a universal, almost instinctual, desire on the part of the viewer to experience balance, rhythm, emphasis, proportion, and harmony. In this family room, two design principles—the use of symmetry and the Golden Mean Principle —create a calming sense of balance.

This family room takes full advantage of
quirky corners and unusual angles to build in a fireplace, television niche, and storage into the room.

*Floating beams create intimacy with-
out closing off the soaring ceilings. At
night, recessed lights from the beams
make the room feel warm and cozy.*

Creative use of space in this basement rec room transforms a small alcove into front-row seating for a pool game. The mirror above the bench seat mimics the idea of a window, just as the built-in bench seat evokes the quaint-ness of a window seat.

*Design*Wise

Tim Quigley, AIA

Quigley Architects
Minneapolis, MN
612-692-8850

SERIOUS SOUND ISOLATION

For home theaters, space for band practice, recording studios, or any space in which sound isolation is important, consider rebuilding the ceiling. Install isolating membrane between the structure (floor joist) and the gypsum board (dry wall).

LIGHT LOCATION

When planning your media room, never place televisions opposite windows. Reflections caused by natural light on your TV screen would make viewing difficult during portions of the day. Also, try not to place recessed lighting, floor lamps, ceiling mounted lighting or track lighting between the viewer and the sreen. Finally, install dimmers on light switches in your media room for optimum viewing conditions.

LIBRARY FOR LESS

The most efficient way to provide a library function without an actual library is to line one or more walls of a room with floor to ceiling bookshelves. For less that $250 and just a few hours of labor you can cover an 8 X 6 wall with shelves. If you don't want to deal with painting or staining and varnish-ing wood shelves, melamine shelves are a sturdy, easier alternative.

When space is tight and you don't want to expand beyond the current footprint, garage conversion can be an attractive option. Here, new flooring and windows transform the white-washed interior of an old garage into a casual, quiet escape.

Window Seats

If we sit perfectly still and stare straight ahead for any length of time, we're likely to be whispered about…unless we're in a window seat. Perched at the perimeter of the outside world, a window seat anchors us; from its safe sanctuary, the mind is set free. This solitary little refuge is insistent: Sit, listen, stare, relax.

Tinted glass reduces glare and limits the fading and other sun damage to the carpet and upholstery, which is particularly important for undraped windows.

Optimal depth for a window seat is 30" to 36". Less that 24" is uncomfortable.

Windows can be combined and arranged to create nooks and crannies filled with light. Here, fixed windows are stacked to create a sunny corner for reading. Nearby casement windows flank a picture window topped by transoms, framing a large, comfortable window seat.

This bench serves several purposes: It's a place to sit down to change into or out of muddy shoes; it's also the best summer reading spot in the house—mosquito-free, a back-door breeze, shade.

Extra storage space!

Built-in benches offer the same statement as window seats: Sit here, relax, no one will bother you for a few minutes.

Nesting tables are convenient where space is tight. They come in all materials—wood, glass, wrought iron, wicker, chrome, aluminum—and at many price points. The height of the tallest table is usually 18" to 24", perfect for placement next to window seats and benches.

Media Centers

"Media center" is the name given to any configuration of technology that delivers audio, moving images, still images, interactive electronics, Internet access, computer functions, or any combination thereof from a centralized location. It can be as complicated or as simple, as cheap or expensive as you desire. It may take up a tiny corner, a single shelf, or an entire room.

Only the need for organized, expandable storage is a constant. Even those of us who don't consider ourselves "collectors" typically end up with more—rather than fewer—CDs, DVDs, and videos over time.

In the following pages, we'll look at several types of media centers, including expandable media centers and specialized cabinets.

Expandable media centers, like this, consist of open and closed shelving that can be reconfigured and expanded over time. It's the most practical option for the young, the inquisitive, and the acquisitive. Adjustable shelving units easily accommodate the ever-changing hardware needs of the budding technophile. A media setup like this can be configured for under $500 (not including any equipment or CDs—shelving and cabinetry only).

Clamp spotlights, at less than $10 each, are inexpensive options for much-needed task lighting on storage shelves.

Highest shelves are designated for "dead" storage–those extras you rarely need to access.

Magazine storage boxes make user manuals as well as magazines easy to locate.

These homeowners can expand and reconfigure this modular media center as their needs change. The total cost for all shelving and cabinetry seen here is less than $900.

To preserve the shelf life of your electronics, leave at least one open inch around all sides of the TV and behind it to allow for adequate ventilation.

CDs and DVDs can be organized by category or in alphabetocal order with these storage units.

Store items that don't stack or line up as neatly as books, and keep CDs out of sight.

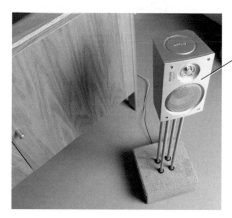

For the best tonal quality, position your speakers so that they are closer to your ears than they are to side walls. You want sound from the speakers to reach your ears before sound reflected from the walls reaches them.

Home theaters provide the ultimate home entertainment experience.

Most home theater systems use five standard speakers plus an optional subwoofer. Ideally, you want three identical full-size front speakers. Place the rear ("surround") speakers above ear level, facing forward, behind the viewer (or to the sides of the viewer facing the viewer).

The cost of a home theater starts at about $1,200 and continues to as high as you care to go. Room design and decoration, screen selection, and lighting conditions all work together to produce a pleasurable experience.

If you're considering a pull-down screen, look for a tab tensioned model, as these tend to remain nice and flat over a longer time period.

The less ambient light, the better the
viewing.
Dark walls are great in home theaters as
they absorb light that might otherwise reflect back and
disturb picture quality. Also, consider investing in heavy
carpeting with good padding beneath it to absorb some
of the heavier sound.

*Home theater designers recommend placing seats
back a distance no less than twice the width of
your screen. Don't, however, push the seats all the
way to the back wall or you'll miss the full beauty
of surround sound.*

A media cabinet should enhance the style of the room

in which it's situated. You can find cabinets in every style from mission to modern, shabby chic, French country, Asian, contemporary—and everything in between.

"Flipper" or "pocket" doors are a great advantage when you want to hide away your media setup. They're hidden when the cabinet is open, and pull straight out (with little clearance room required) when it's time to close the cabinet.

Fixed cabinet media centers

don't flow quite as easily with technology changes as do modular systems. The upside of single-piece cabinets is that they're often much better looking, more refined, and far more visually creative than their modular counterparts.

Libraries

The love of learning, the sequestered nooks,
And all the sweet serenity of books.
— Henry Wadsworth Longfellow (1807 - 1882)

Attention all bibliophiles: In a survey just released, the National Association of Homebuilders (NAHB) found that more homeowners expressed an interested in having a den/library (54 percent) than in a separate media room (28percent). No, our love of TV, DVD, iPOD, TiVo, and related acronyms has not managed to squelch our first media love, the book.

Natural light pouring in from the paneled glass

at right gives this library/den incredible warmth. Sunlight adds vibrancy to even the most muted, understated earth tones.

To safeguard rare, older books and other items that can't tolerate dust, consider shelves with glass-paneled doors.

Every good book deserves a window seat. Many older homes come with heavy cast iron radiators below the windows. These are actually window seats waiting to happen. Happily, you need nothing more than a plank and a pillow.

The ideal home library combines a variety of shelving, seating, and lighting.

Shelving units with an overhang on the top beg for under-cabinet lighting.

Provide a separate standing lamp or other source of task lighting for each seat in the library.

Build your library wherever space allows. If space is tight, utilize the area under the stairs or on a landing. Narrow, adjustable shelves anchored to wall studs can host a surprisingly large library.

Playrooms

The biggest challenge in designing a playroom for kids is that nothing works for more than a few years. From toddlerhood on, children and their belongings, interests, and preferences are a moving target, and playrooms must accommodate this constant evolution.

Another factor that goes into playroom design is whether you want to separate the area, giving the kids maximum freedom to splatter paint and use their outside voices, or whether you prefer to have the children close by so you can keep an eye on them and interact regularly.

The issue of how to set up a playroom intersects with core beliefs about parenting. Take a few minutes to really think through these issues:

- What do my children need?
- What are my needs vis-à-vis the children's needs?
- What floor do I want them on?
- What indoor activities are appropriate?
- What's the best way for our family to find that compromise between the adult need for a bit of order, and our kids' need to spread their wings, raise their voices, and…just be kids?

There's no one right answer.

Hooks with no sharp or hard edges are safe for kids and make it easy to keep rooms tidy.

Choose durable, easy-to-clean wall and floor treatments.

They're only young once. Indulge a child's desire for colors you would not otherwise choose. Use gloss or semi-gloss paint.

Carpeting can be difficult to maintain in a playroom. Instead, choose scrubbable floor coverings and washable area rugs.

Any durable, sturdy storage device on wheels is great in a playroom.

Nesting play tables—a wonderful advantage in smaller rooms!

Chalkboards and rolls of drawing paper legalize every child's penchant for drawing on the wall.

*Idea*Wise

PAPER-ON-A-ROLL

In this day of technology and carefully scheduled activities, it's nice to give a child a place to sit quietly and create. Attaching a large roll of butcher paper to an old table is a simple, inexpensive way to provide a continuous surface for paints, markers, and other media.

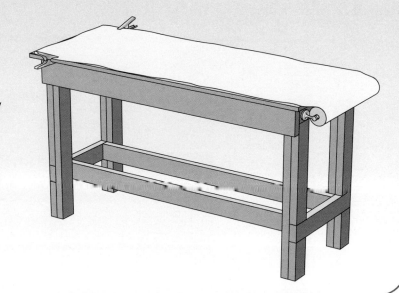

Attach brackets to a sturdy table, positioned to allow plenty of room for creativity. These brackets, as well as multi-colored paper, are available on-line as well as art supply stores.

Attics and basements offer relative privacy and seclusion

Attics are out of the traffic patterns of the house; noise is muffled from below; and other people in the house are less likely to interrupt the attic denizen (out of sight, out of mind).

Family treasures and other mementos are displayed on simple shelves running from the floor to just below the ceiling; deep, intense color warms the room, keeping it from feeling impossibly large.

Skylights add wonderful diffuse light, but they must be placed carefully. In hot climates, avoid south- or west-facing skylights or choose units that can be shaded in the afternoon.

A kneewall is a short wall that meets the slope of the roofline in an upstairs room. By cutting a hole in a kneewall and installing a recessed cabinet, you can turn the wasted space behind it into a useful storage or shelving.

The window you see in this basement room is an egress,
or escape, window. Egress windows must meet code requirements:

- The windowsill must be no more than 44" from the floor.
- The window opening must be no less than 5.7 square feet of space.
- Window height of the window cannot measure less than 24".
- Window width cannot be less than 20".

Most building codes require that basement bedrooms include egress windows.

Even if your plans don't include a bedroom, you may want to install an egress win-

dow if you need more natural light for the space.

*Planters built into the well provide
obvious aesthetic benefit. Large sliding
windows make it easy to let in fresh air.*

Saunas

If sweating helps you relax, you must think seriously about a home sauna. They're only moderately difficult to install. Unlike a steam bath, there is no plumbing or floor drain required. Saunas use dry heat and require 110-volt household current. All you need are a few square feet, some basic electrical hookups, and ceramic tile or concrete for the sauna floor.

Search the Internet for sauna kits; you'll find sizes ranging from 3 × 4 ft. to 12 × 12 ft. at prices that vary widely. The most affordable kits have hemlock, spruce, and fir interiors. Pricier kits feature cedar or redwood walls, and amenities such as light fixtures, back rests, towel bars, and timing controls.

Quiet Spaces

Quiet space has no noise: auditory, visual, or psychological. It's where your eyes rest on something calming, and you hear only what you wish to hear; it's where your mind has a chance—no matter how brief—to stop its incessant thinking. Quiet looks different for different people. It may be a small, dark nook under the stairs, or an open, airy loft-like space, or something else entirely. This is about *your* notion of quiet—whatever that is.

Wall sconces controlled by a dimmer provide soft, reflected light. Dimmers allow a lighting range equivalent to a spectrum from bright daylight to candlelight.

For a quiet space, choose colors that invoke a sense of spiritual stillness. This will be warm tones for some; cool tones for others. Don't worry about color trends—these change all the time. Find the tones that reflect your aesthetic and meet your needs.

For many people, quiet space is neutral and spare.

In this room, simple lines, unadorned walls, and soft, solid colors

produce a tranquil atmosphere.

Resource Guide

A listing of resources for information, designs, and products found in *IdeaWise Activity Spaces*.

Introduction

page 11:
cabinets, furnishings, and accessories by **IKEA**
To shop, request a catalog, or find a store near you, call
1-800-434-4532
or visit www.IKEA.com

Home Offices

Home Offices (cont.)

page 32-33 (both): home office furnishings and accessories by
California Closets
To shop, request a catalog, or find a store near you, call
1-800-274-6754
or visit www.calclosets.com

page 36-37: home office design, furnishings, and accessories by **IKEA**
To shop, request a catalog, or find a store near you, call
1-800-434-4532
or visit www.IKEA.com

page 38: home office storage by
Mill's Pride
2 Easton Oval, Suite 310
Columbus, OH 43219
1-800-441-0337
Mill's Pride cabinets available exclusively at Home Depot
www.millspride.com

page 39: under-cabinet lighting by
California Closets
To shop, request a catalog, or find a store near you, call
1-800-274-6754
or visit www.calclosets.com

page 40: home office design, furnishings, and accessories by **IKEA**
To shop, request a catalog, or find a store near you, call
1-800-434-4532
or visit www.IKEA.com

Specialty Workspaces

page 68:   shelving products manufactured by elfa® International and distributed by **elfa**
elfa® North America
500 Freeport Pkwy.
Coppell, TX 75019-3863
For product information
call 1-800-394-3532
or visit www.elfa.com

page 73 (above):   storage products by **California Closets**
To shop, request a catalog, or find a store near you, call 1-800-274-6754
or visit www.calclosets.com

page 73:   *Design*Wise tips contributed by Susan Nackers Ludwig
Rehkamp Larson Architects, Inc.
Minneapolis, MN
612-285-7275

page 74:   shelving products manufactured by elfa® International and distributed by **elfa**
elfa® North America
500 Freeport Pkwy.
Coppell, TX 75019-3863
For product information
1-800-394-3532
or visit www.elfa.com

page 77:   floor sink by **Kohler**
Kohler products available at showrooms and retailers worldwide. To locate a showroom or retailer near you, call 1-800-456-4537
or visit www.us.kohler.com

Laundry and Mud Rooms

page 66:   family studio design and appliances by **Whirlpool**
To request a catalog or find a store near you,
call 1-800-253-1301
or visit www.whirlpool.com

page 67:   cabinets by
Plato Woodwork, Inc.
Plato, MN 55370
For more information
call 1-800-328-5924 or visit www.platowoodworking.com

Arts, Crafts and Hobbies

page 87:

lamp by
Daylight Company, LLC
Service Center
116 King Court Industrial Park
PO Box 422
New Holland, PA 17557-0422
1-866-DAYLIGHT (329-5444)
www.us.daylightcompany.com

page 90:

cabinets by
Merillat Industries
5353 West US 223
Adrian, MI 49221
To request a catalog or
find a store near you visit
www.merillat.com

page 91:

*Design*Wise tips contributed
by Rosemary McMonigal, AIA
McMonigal Architects
Minneapolis, MN
612-331-1244

page 97:

garden window by
**JELD-WEN® Windows
and Doors**
401 Harbor Isles Blvd.
Klamath Falls, OR 97601
To request a catalog or
find a store near you,
call 1-800-535-3936
or visit www.jeld-wen.com

Relaxation

page 121:   design, furnishings, and
               accessories by **IKEA**
               To shop, request a catalog, or
               find a store near you, call
               1-800-434-4532
               or visit www.IKEA.com

page 122:   design, furnishings, and
               accessories by **IKEA**
               To shop, request a catalog, or
               find a store near you, call
               1-800-434-4532
               or visit www.IKEA.com

page 125:   egress window and
               scapeWEL Window Well by
               The Bilco Company
               P.O. Box 1203
               New Haven CT 06505
               www.bilco.com

page 126-127 (both): sauna by
               Finnleo Sauna & Steam
               Cokato, MN
               for more information call
               1-800-FINNLEO
               or visit www.finnleo.com

Additional Resources

INTERNATIONAL CODE COUNCIL (ICC)

www.iccsafe.org
The International Code Council (ICC) was established in 1994 as a nonprofit organization dedicated to developing a single set of national construction codes in the following areas: Building, plumbing, fire, mechanical, energy conservation, zoning, electrical, and others. They also offer the following services:
- Code application assistance
- Educational programs
- Certification programs
- Technical handbooks and workbooks
- Plan reviews
- Automated products
- Monthly magazines and newsletters
- Publication of proposed code changes
- Training and informational videos
- Consumer and safety tips

ICC OFFICES

Headquarters
5203 Leesburg Pike, Suite 600
Falls Church, VA 22041
703-931-4533

Birmingham District Office
900 Montclair Rd.
Birmingham, AL 35213
205-591-1853

Chicago District Office
4051 W. Flossmoor Rd.
Country Club Hills, IL 60478
1-800-214-4321

Los Angeles District Office
5360 Workman Mill Rd.
Whittier, CA 90601
1-800-284-4406

ICC SUBSIDIARIES

ICC Evaluation Service Business/Regional Office
5360 Workman Mill Rd.
Whittier, CA 90601
562-699-0543

Regional Office
900 Montclair Rd., Suite A
Birmingham, AL 35213
205-599-9800

Regional Office
4051 West Flossmoor Rd.
Country Club Hills, IL 60478
708-799-2305

International Accreditation Service
5360 Workman Mill Rd.
Whittier, CA 90601
562-699-0541

International Code Council Foundation
PO Box 11335
Cincinnati, OH 45211
513-574-0957

CONSUMER REPORTS

Customer Relations Department
101 Truman Ave.
Yonkers, NY 10703
www.consumerreports.org

www.consumerreports.org is the place to go if you're contemplating an appliance, computer, or electronics purchase.
www.consumerreports.org is an independent nonprofit organization whose mission is to work for a fair, just, and safe marketplace for all consumers and to empower consumers to protect themselves. They perform expert testing on thousands of products in the following categories:

Appliances
Refrigerators, washers, dishwashers, dryers, vacuum cleaners.

Electronics & computers
Cell phones, digital cameras, TVs, PDAs, laptops, camcorders.

Home & garden
Air conditioners, grills, deck treatments, lawn mowers & tractors.

Health & fitness
Exercise & diet, treadmills, dangerous supplements.

NATIONAL ASSOCIATION OF HOME BUILDERS (NAHB)

1201 15th St., NW
Washington, DC 20005-2800
1-800-368-5242
www.nahb.org

The National Association of Home Builders is an excellent resource for information, education, research, technical expertise, economic and housing data, codes & standards, and finding remodelers/builders in your area.

OTHER RESOURCES

Black & Decker®
The Complete Guide to Home Carpentry: Carpentry Skills & Projects for the Homeowner

Black & Decker®
The Complete Guide to Home Storage: More Than 50 Practical Projects & Ideas

Black & Decker®
The Complete Guide to Windows & Doors: Step-by-Step Projects for Adding, Replacing & Repairing All Types of Windows and Doors

Black & Decker®
The Complete Guide to Easy Woodworking Projects: 50 Projects & Ideas

Photo Credits

front cover and title page:
Photo courtesy of IKEA.

back cover: (top left) Photo courtesy of Koechel Peterson &
Associates for Plato Woodwork, Inc.; (top right) ©Getty Images;
(bottom left) Finnleo Sauna and Steam/finnleo.com;
(bottom center) Photo courtesy of California Closets/calclosets.com;
(bottom right) Photo courtesy of IKEA.

pp. 2-3: (top) ©Andrea Rugg for Awad & Koontz Architect Builders,
Inc.; (bottom left) ©Getdecorating.com; (bottom right) ©Andrea Rugg
for Schrock & DeVetter Architects.

pp. 4-5: ©image/Dennis Krukowski for Libby Cameron, LLC,
Larchmont, NY.

p. 7: ©image/Dennis Krukowski for Joanna Seitz New Preston, CT.

pp. 8-9: (both) ©Jessie Walker.

p. 11: Photo courtesy of IKEA.

p. 12: ©Getty Images.

p. 15: ©Andrea Rugg/Beateworks.com.

p. 16: (top) ©Karen Melvin; (bottom) ©Jessie Walker.

p. 17: (top) ©Getdecorating.com; (bottom) Photo courtesy of IKEA.

p. 18: ©Karen Melvin for Sala Architects.

p. 19: (top) ©Karen Melvin; (bottom) ©Beateworks.com.

p. 20: (top) ©Jessie Walker; (bottom) ©Tim Street-Porter
/Beateworks.com.

p. 21: (top) Photo courtesy of California Closets/calclosets.com;
(bottom) Photo courtesy of IKEA.

p. 22: (both) ©Tim Street-Porter/Beateworks.com.

p. 23: Photo courtesy of California Closets/calclosets.com.

p. 26: (top) ©Karen Melvin for Harold Peterson.

p.27: (top) ©Brand X Pictures; (bottom) ©William Geddes/
Beateworks.com.

p. 28: Photo courtesy of Mill's Pride.

p. 29: Photo Courtesy of IKEA.

p. 30: ©William Geddes/Beateworks.com.

p. 31: Tim Street-Porter/Beateworks.com.

pp. 32-33: Photo courtesy of California Closets/calclosets.com.

p. 35: (top) ©Jessie Walker; (bottom) ©Douglas Hill/
Beateworks.com.

pp. 36-37: (top) ©Karen Melvin for Paragon Designers & Builders,
Ramsey Enler, Ltd., and SKD Architects; (bottom) Photo courtesy of IKEA.

p. 38: Photo courtesy of Mill's Pride.

p. 39: Photo courtesy of California Closets/calclosets.com.

p. 40: Photo courtesy of IKEA.

p. 41: ©Getdecorating.com.

p. 42: Photo courtesy of Kraftmaid Cabinetry, Inc.

p. 44: Photos courtesy of Mill's Pride.

p. 45: Photo Courtesy of Binkys Woodworking/
binkyswoodworking.com.

p. 46: Photo Courtesy of Binkys Woodworking/
binkyswoodworking.com.

p. 47: (top) Photo Courtesy of Binkys Woodworking/
binkyswoodworking.com; (bottom) Photo courtesy of Mill's Pride.

p. 48: (top) Photo courtesy of California Closets/calclosets.com.

p. 50: ©Andrea Rugg.

p. 52: ©J. Scott Smith/Beateworks.com.

p. 53: Photo courtesy of IKEA.

p. 54: ©Karen Melvin for Sound and Image Magazine.

p. 55: ©Getdecorating.com.

pp. 56-57: ©Getdecorating.com.

pp. 58-59: (both) ©Getdecorating.com.

p. 60: ©Getty Images.

p. 62: ©Getdecorating.com.

p. 63: ©Karen Melvin for Jenn Air Appliances.

p. 64: ©Getdecorating.com.

p. 65: ©Jessie Walker.

pp. 66-67: Photos courtesy of Whirlpool Appliances.

p. 68: Photo courtesy of elfa® North America. Shelving Products
manufactured by elfa® International, AB distributed by elfa®
North America.

p. 69: (both) ©Jessie Walker.

p. 70: ©Karen Melvin.

p. 71: ©Jessie Walker.

p. 72: (both) ©Karen Melvin; (top) for Ginny Anderson Architect;
(bottom) for Three Studios Architects, Rick Lundin Architect.

p. 73: Photo courtesy of California Closets/calclosets.com.

p. 74: Photo courtesy of elfa® North America. Shelving Products
manufactured by elfa® International, AB distributed by elfa®
North America.

p.75: ©Karen Melvin for Mason Homes.

p. 76: ©Andrea Rugg for Rehkamp Larson Architects, Inc.

p. 77 Photo courtsy of Kohler Co.

Index

Also from

CREATIVE PUBLISHING INTERNATIONAL

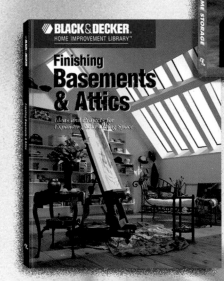

ISBN 0-86573-577-8

ISBN 0-86573-581-6

ISBN 0-86573-583-2

CREATIVE PUBLISHING INTERNATIONAL

18705 LAKE DRIVE EAST
CHANHASSEN, MN 55317

WWW.CREATIVEPUB.COM